The Tiny Book of Love

BOOK OF KATHERINE

ISBN: 979-8-9990512-3-3

Cover design by Book of Katherine
Cover photo by Dhanya Purohit
Back cover photo by Amith Tiwari

THE TINY BOOK SERIES
By Book of Katherine

THE TINY BOOK OF FASHION
The quick and dirty answers to
fashion's deepest questions.

THE TINY BOOK OF LOVE
Love isn't where you think you'll find it.
But it can be found.

THE TINY BOOK OF NATURE
Justice is all around us.
And court is in session.

What's love got to do with it?
Tina Turner

Where there is life there is hope.
J.R.R. Tolkien

CONTENTS

CHAPTER ONE
LOVE AIN'T WORTH SHIT

All day long, from the day we are born, we are told, sold and molded into believing that love is absolutely everything. We are told we must strive for it. We are told we will die without it.

Bullshit.

Life.

Life is the real ball-buster.

And until we make life the center of all our pursuits, studies and goals, then we are seriously fucked as a society and as individuals...

As one can plainly see if we bother to look around and pay attention for a change.

CHAPTER TWO
LIFE: THE ULTIMATE THREAT

You can pursue love all damn day, and no one will stop you. Oh, parents may wail and say that you have failed them because you haven't brought in the other thing we are programmed to live and die for: money and power thinly veiled behind the term success. But they will go full-mental if you pursue life.

And that's because life is the ultimate curse breaker. Seek life and you seek the kingdom of God itself.

It's just as dangerous as pursuing truth, because life and truth are the same.

CHAPTER THREE
THE WAR

It sounds strange, doesn't it?

Oh, my sons and daughters! Sisters and brothers! Pursue passion! Pursue love! Pursue purpose! Go out! Procreate! Multiply!

Yeah. The people who say that kind of shit in their Hallmark movie scripts, romance novels, pulpits and meditation retreats are the very same ones who will put a bullet in your brain for telling their flocks to pursue life and - *gasp!* - truth.

You wouldn't think there'd be a war between the Life-and-Truth camp and the Love-and-Passion camp, but there is, especially when the Love-and-Passion camp is making a great deal of money off its message.

For their version of pursuing love and passion requires money.

And lots of it.
Pursuing life and truth?
Not so much.

CHAPTER FOUR
TRY IT

Go ahead and try it.

Try switching from the pursuit of *love and happiness* to the pursuit of *life and truth* for just one day and see how that goes.

Do you even know how?

I mean, you'll have to put down the cologne, the cosmetics, the phone with all your dating apps and even – dare I say it! – leave behind the gargantuan collection of stuff you've collected in that pursuit of love and happiness over the years.

Can you do that?

Do you think you can survive?

I think you'll thrive.

CHAPTER FIVE
THE PURSUIT OF LIFE
(AND MAYBE SOME TRUTH TOO)

Life is easy to find. We're just not used to recognizing it, never mind pursuing it.

Life can be found in your friends, your family, your pets, your plants, the wind, the trees, the brook, the breeze.

Look around you. Notice what is alive.

Notice what isn't.

And remember what you spend most of your time with.

That's some hard truth right there.

It hurts.

But fuck it.

Wouldn't you rather know?

CHAPTER SIX
NOW CHASE IT

Recognizing life is only the first step.

But the most important step comes next: the *pursuit* of it.

Just noticing what is alive and what isn't - well - that doesn't constitute chasing anything at all, does it? That just means you're noticing what's alive.

And the act of noticing, although invaluable in so many situations, is passive in its nature. It's neutral.

And you can't be neutral when you pursue something. Otherwise it will pass you by.

Oh, no. You need to *chase* it.

Chase life!

Run it down!

Pursue it!

So. You just realized that a little blade of grass has managed to live, despite all the concrete, tar and poisons along your block.

Well, what are you going to do next?

Stare at it?

No! Draw it! Sketch it! Water it! Talk to it, for fuck's sake, if you have to!

I certainly do!

I talk to all of my living things where I live... and you may think that's crazy, but let me tell you – I'm the one with the property people call enchanted.

When I pull up into my driveway, the birds fly next to my car while the squirrels run out to greet me. (And no, I'm not offering them any nuts!) I post videos of these happenings all the time. People ask why everything living – the deer, the horses, even the emus! – approach me or pose when I start filming.

Haven't you ever noticed that I am always talking to them? Do you really think that's just a freaky coincidence?

Or do you think that's because I fuckin' *pursue* life!?

Whether it's human or not!?

Yes, yes, yes. That was a rhetorical question. Of course the land comes alive when I acknowledge its life.

And that's a form of love few are familiar with. But there's a reason it always appears in the stories and fables about true love.

CHAPTER SEVEN

SPEAKING OF
GOD'S CREATURES

I'm not saying that you should speak to the animals around you. I'm just saying that it wouldn't hurt.

There are many ways to pursue life, and if you do it right, you will find yourself in the pursuit of truth as well.

How does one pursue life right? Well, for one thing, I'd avoid artificial forms of life if you can. For example, I wouldn't go to a zoo unless there was absolutely nothing else living anywhere near you (which I highly doubt).

Instead, look for life that's living unencumbered.

Look for life in its most natural state.

I'll never forget the day I sat on the beach in Hawaii watching my much younger sister play with the waves lapping at the shore. She was in another world, as surprise-siblings often are. But oh! What a world she was in!

My instinct was to leave her alone and observe her. I tried to listen closely and find the world she was experiencing. She was full of life – joy! – curiosity and excitement.

The life surged off of her like I'd never seen, so free was she, so enamored of that magical shoreline… and I knew that in order to soak up that exuberance of hers, I was required to stay silent.

I watched her fingers brush the bubbles of the blue frothy waves tickling her feet. She spoke to them, as though entire worlds existed in each bubble, and she was inviting them to come out and play.

I could see a rhythm and a rhyme to her dance. For she did – she danced. She tickled one wave here, whispered to another there, and the glory of that Hawaiian sunset illuminated the holiness of her revelry.

She was a sprite, enveloped in a world long forgotten… but the longer she danced, the more I could see. And I was in awe.

But then my parents interrupted her. They wanted to normalize her. They made her sit down and be silent. They shut her up like a storybook, never to be opened again.

I never saw the life pour off of her like that again. The next year, when we visited that same beach for the very last time, she never even left my mother's side – the life in her tamed into submission.

Today she is locked up tight with a long set of algorithms running in her head. She is full of programming that someone else wrote. She isn't her own. She is a script.

And as such, she isn't unique.

She isn't alive.

And I don't want that for you.

I don't want that for me.

I want to live.

refuses to allow his tabernacle to be set up in the middle of the camp of the twelve Hebrew tribes because, as he puts it, their evil would've made him want to burn them up on the spot.

Instead, the Lord asked Moses and Aaron to set up his tabernacle outside of the encampment of his people.

In fact, he asked that his home be placed on the eastern edge of the encampment, so that he'd be the first to see the Sun come up every day. That's how desperate the Lord was to seek life in that camp – he literally moved towards the Sun!

And Jesus!? Have you read the *Gospel of Matthew: Chapter 23*!? It contains what's called *The Eight Woes*. At every sermon throughout the gospels, the academics, pastors and rabbis of the day quiz him. Jesus usually gives them a single sentence answer.

But in the end, he snaps. And he spends an entire chapter just nailing these guys.

What guys? Why, the same ones we have today! Recognize them? This is how Jesus describes them:

Their lives are perpetual fashion shows, embroidered prayer shawls one day and flowery prayers the next. They love to sit at the head table at church dinners, basking in the most prominent positions, preening in the radiance of public flattery, receiving honorary degrees, and getting called 'Doctor' and 'Reverend.'

-Gospel of Matthew 23:5-7 (MSG)
After calling them out, Jesus then rains down eight curses against them, which we now call *The Eight Woes.*

And it is here that I believe Jesus actually curses. Yup! He used what would've been considered bad words back then, so angry was he at their insistence on locking people up tight instead of setting them free, no matter how many sermons of his they attended, or how much access they had to being in the Lord's very presence in what was then the third and final temple (aka Herod's Temple).

Oh yes – those guys really pissed him off. And they pissed me off too.

They still do!

They are the same people telling us all to work our asses off all our lives pursuing love instead of pursuing life right now.

Instead of giving you God's Law as food and drink by which you can banquet on God, they package it in bundles of rules, loading you down like pack animals. They seem to take pleasure in watching you stagger under these loads, and wouldn't think of lifting a finger to help.

-Gospel of Matthew 23:4 (MSG)
Oh, yes. Every culture has to put up with their own version of these people even now, 2000 years later. I've been counting embroidered shawls ever since reading this passage – and it's astounding just how many varieties there are.

And it's astounding how much sway an embroidered shawl has. Sigh. No.

They didn't go away, sadly.

Poo.

CHAPTER NINE
AFTER LIFE

Once you find life, once you taste it, once you get to know it and recognize it and feel it before it crosses your line of sight – then you will find that your perspective on love has begun to change.

And that's because, by pursuing life, you've stopped pursuing death.

That's what those death dealers are peddling, you know, when they tell you you're nothing because you haven't found 'the one' yet.

Not all of us are designed for another! Even Jesus himself says that! He says marriage is lofty and hard as hell and not for everyone – and he even warns against going into it just because others want you to.

Oh, no.

When there is someone you were born for,

you know it when you meet. It's not always apparent at the outset, but sometimes it happens immediately.

Either way, everyone around you can see it – you both glow when you're near one another, and you both begin to make your own way – your own path as one – in the world.

Now, to be fair, unhealthy relationships can mimic this sometimes. But look for the red flags. When two are meant to be together, they make each other stronger. Both grow bolder. Both become more mature.

Both simply grow.

And they are vulnerable with one another – thoughtful.

Fear. Fear is the big indicator when it comes to love bombing and unhealthy codependency that eventually destroys a relationship, despite appearing shiny and bright to the outside world.

If a partner is scared of disappointing their girlfriend or boyfriend, or they change their behavior just to please them – especially their dress – then those are red flags.

A heaven-sent match helps us become who we are more fully, not change who we are.

And it's hard sometimes.

Sometimes we find out that our friends aren't really that likable when they find someone that fits them perfectly. It turns out that they've been sitting on some pretty ugly opinions and outlooks sometimes.

But it's better to know than not know in such cases.

Or perhaps that's just my love of the truth that's talking...

CHAPTER 10
LIES ABOUT LOVE

Before I go, I want to address one famous quote about love. It's in the Bible and people who say they love Jesus will usually know this quote better than they know what Jesus himself has said about love.

The very pastors and religious academics Jesus railed against in the *Gospel of Matthew: Chapter 23* are the very ones who do not teach about what Jesus says at all – despite hoisting a massive cross up on their building's walls.

Instead, these vultures, as Jesus calls them in *Matthew 24*, they teach what a guy named Paul wrote instead. He was from a city of Roman Pharisees. He grew up studying Greek and Roman philosophers, not just the Hebrew texts.

And man, it shows.

Paul wrote a lot of shit.

For example, Paul called himself an apostle. But he wasn't. Jesus chose the first twelve apostles from among his closest followers. When the one known as Judas took his own life after betraying Jesus, the other eleven apostles elected Matthias to take the twelfth spot, not Paul.

Paul didn't even bother to show up when Jesus was in town.

He didn't even show up for a full year after Jesus ascended into heaven! And when he did, he led a stoning against one of the twelve chosen: Stephen.

But here's the problem.

The apostles were trained in how to raise people from the dead. I don't know why anyone who believes in Jesus thinks that any of the twelve apostles died.

Judas died because he hung himself. He chose to leave.

And the other eleven didn't know where he was to raise him from the dead.

Instead, the other twelve were raising people from the dead just like Jesus did with Lazarus! And – here's the kicker – Jesus actually told his disciples that they would live until his return.

So unless that's happened – unless Jesus has returned? Those twelve are still kicking. I wouldn't be surprised.

But then again, I've spent my years in the pursuit of life. I've learned a thing or two about it.

And it's not the fairy tales we've been fed. Life is a wild and untamed thing – it's crazy – chaotic – and yet orderly at the same time.

And I love.

But anyhow – back to the famous quote that the liar Paul wrote (you know he just plagiarized the teachings of the Romans and the Greeks, right?).

You'll find this quote in Paul's first letter to the Corinthians:

Love is patient, love is kind. It does not envy, it does not boast, it is not proud. It does not dishonor others, it is not self-seeking, it is not easily angered, it keeps no record of wrongs. Love does not delight in evil but rejoices with the truth. It always protects, always trusts, always, hopes, always perseveres. Love never fails.

-1 Corinthians 13:4-8 (NIV)

Oh give me a break.

Do you know what a guilt trip this quote puts people on!? I mean – if I'm not patient, that means I'm not loving!? Are you fucking kidding me? Does a mother in labor not love her child when she's impatiently waiting for them to get the fuck out of her already!?

And love doesn't always hope! It doesn't always persevere! Love is sticky and messy and crazy and chaotic – just like life!

But Paul is plagiarizing the Greek and Roman philosophers, remember? And their goal was to control the slaves. And boy, oh boy, do these words play a large role in the creation and control of our self-imposed slavery today.

CHAPTER 11
TRUE LOVE

True love has boundaries. When in love, you can tell the person to fuck off without worrying that they will leave you. Love never leaves.

Love never, ever leaves, even when it feels like it.

And love exists outside of romance. There are more kinds of love than there are stars in the sky. For where there is light, there is life. And where there is life, there is hope. And where there is hope… there is love.

You are loved.

If you take away anything from this tiny book, take away this: I love you.

I love you even though I haven't met you. But you are alive.

And fuck it, you have done things. I know you have. But I still love you.

And if I, I who has never met you, can love you just knowing that you breathe – then you can love too.

It may not seem like it. It may not feel like it.

But love is more often than not an act, not a feeling.

CHAPTER 12

FREEDOM

There is only one nation on earth that ever gave its people the freedom of speech: the United States of America. And though that right has been warred against and attacked ever since it was born, it was born nonetheless.

And it made those who wrote and signed the *Declaration of Independence* some of the most infamous, influential and hated persons in history. But no matter where you stand on the matter, most citizens of the United States say that they believe in the *Bill of Rights*, no matter which party or side they belong to.

And the *Bill of Rights* was introduced into the world through the following opening:

We hold these truths to be sacred & undeniable; that all men are created equal & independent, that from that equal creation they derive rights inherent

& inalienable, among which are the preservation
of life, liberty & the pursuit of happiness…
Life. Liberty. The pursuit of happiness.
Love is not mentioned.
The preservation of life is.

EPILOGUE
THE LIFE WITHIN US

Oh, my friends. I bet you thought that my first tiny book, *The Tiny Book of Fashion*, was scandalous.

And yet here I am, managing to be scandalous about something we're all supposed to be agreed upon! Love!

Funny how that works.

And I suppose one might think that finding one's own Look in fashion goes directly against what I've written here in these twelve chapters. But I'm going to let you in on a little secret: these two books actually go hand in hand.

For *The Tiny Book of Fashion* teaches you to pursue your own life. I didn't mention that, did I, when I listed what is around that's living? I didn't mention *you*.

You are alive.

And that is a miracle. Look down at the inside of your wrist, where you try on color swatches and lipstick trends, where you clasp your watch or put on a weekend wristband. Lying there beneath all those tasks is a pulse. And it beats, on and on and on... a strong sign of life that's always with you.

But how do you pursue the life within you? The tasks I lay out in *The Tiny Book of Fashion* are just one avenue of doing so – for no one is excited in quite the same way. No one feels a personal connection to every piece in a store.

Oh, no. To find your Look is to pursue the very life that beats within your veins. And notice! I don't simply suggest analyzing what you love in a store or gallery. I suggest going outdoors and yes – studying living things around us too.

It's been a hard lesson to learn, but I think Solomon surrounded by all of his gold statues and all of his exotic fabrics from far off cultures never could hold a candle to a single hot-pink bougainvillea flower.

Art only imitates life.

But we sure as hell bring out the life within us when we make it!

ACKNOWLEDGEMENTS
THE LOVES OF MY LIFE

One of my favorite quotes about love comes from one of the twelve Chosen, John:

"Everyone who loves is born of God and experiences a relationship with God. The person who refuses to love doesn't know the first thing about God, because God is love – so you can't know him if you don't love."

-1 John 4 (MSG)

We are often told that heaven and hell are separated by the words we say, the rhetoric we choose, the clothes we wear and the rules we live by.

But John tells us that the world is divided by those who love and those who do not love.

It hasn't been easy. I've made many a hard choice, most of them quite unconventional. But in the end, the result has been life – the very miracle of life itself – and a life full of truth, love, joy and freedom too.

And that is what pulls me through the pain. For life is painful. It simply is. And the lies about love only make that pain so much worse.

But in seeking life, I have found myself both in love and loved in ways unimaginable. Heaven makes sense. Love songs ring true. And every time I think I know what love is, I rediscover it all over again, and I find myself humbled and amazed at its glory.

This book would not exist if it were not for them — for those who love me. I do not deserve them. But I love them so very, very much. I owe my life to them.

All of them.

You have opened my eyes, nursed me back to health and taught me the nature of love in gentle tones, explosive groans, bolts of lightning, waves crashing and in the still of the night, when I thought no one was listening.

I am forever in your debt. Thank you.

www.ingramcontent.com/pod-product-compliance
Lightning Source LLC
Chambersburg PA
CBHW022135280326
41933CB00007B/698